Pom-Pom Whimsy

Crafty kids will have loads of fun making and playing with these whimsical pom-pom crafts. Every project begins with purchased pom-poms and takes just minutes to make. Kids will love making their projects extra special with all the bright, colorful, fluffy, soft pom-poms. So gather the kids and supplies and make a menagerie of pom-pom projects!

LEISURE ARTS, INC.
Maumelle, Arkansas

Table of Contents

Size Guides

Pom poms, also known as poms, come in a variety of sizes; here's a handy size chart that will help you when picking pom poms for a project.

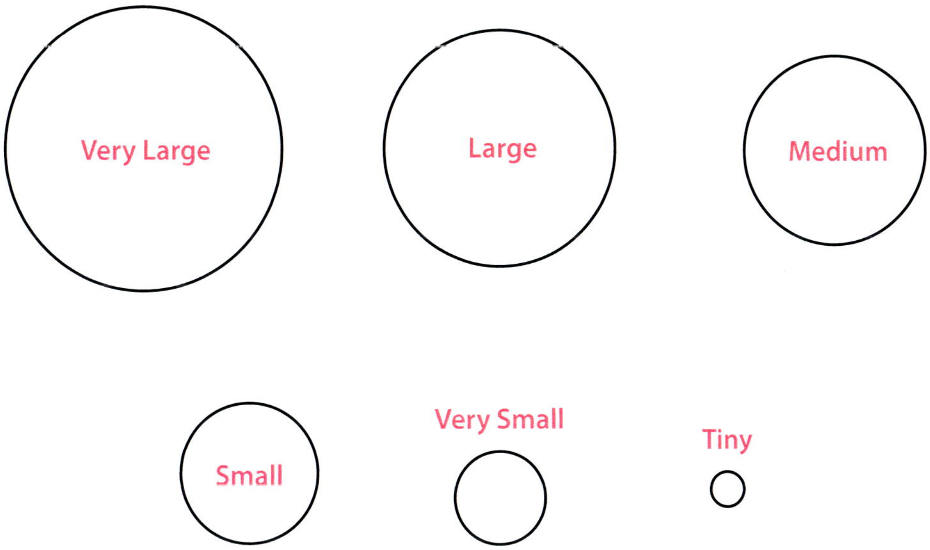

Wiggle eyes also come in a variety of sizes; here's a size chart for those.

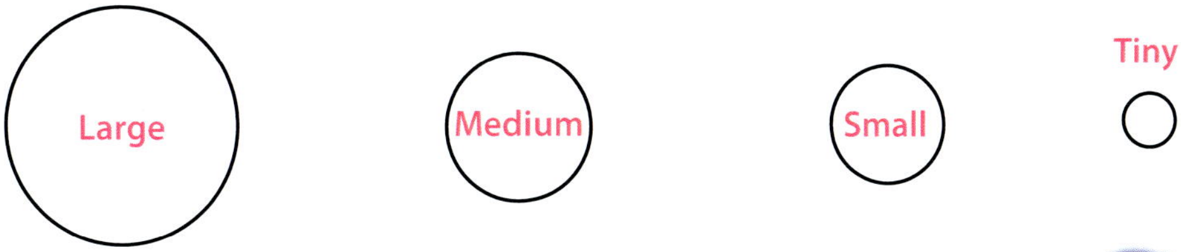

See our broad selection of **Essentials by Leisure Arts** pom poms, chenille stems, and wiggle eyes at www.leisurearts.com.

Swamp Critters

SHOPPING LIST

ALLIGATOR

- ☐ green pom poms (3 large, 5 small, 8 very small, and 2 tiny)
- ☐ 2 small wiggle eyes
- ☐ craft glue

GIANT BUG

- ☐ lime green pom poms (1 very large and 1 medium)
- ☐ 1 very small black pom pom
- ☐ black and neon green chenille stems
- ☐ 2 small wiggle eyes
- ☐ craft glue

Be sure to refer to the Size Guides on page 3 before starting your project.

To make the Alligator:

1. Refer to Fig. 1 to glue the large, small, and 4 very small green poms together for the head, body, and tail.

Fig. 1

2. For legs, glue 4 very small poms to the body. Glue the wiggle eyes to the eye poms. Glue the tiny poms to the snout.

To make the Giant Bug:

1. Glue the lime green poms together. Cut an 11" piece each of neon green and black chenille stems. Twist stems together and shape into a figure 8 for the wings. Glue the center of the wings to the bug body.

2. For the legs, cut two $4^1/_2$" pieces of black chenille stem. Hold both pieces together and twist together at the middle. Separate the chenille stems into 2 legs on each side. Shape the legs and bend the ends to make feet. Glue to the body.

3. For the stinger, cut a 4" piece of black chenille stem. Fold in half and glue to the head. Glue the wiggle eyes to the head.

4. For the tail, cut a 2" piece of black chenille stem. Curl around a pencil and glue to the body. Glue the black pom on the end.

Continued on page 6.

Swamp Critters, continued

SHOPPING LIST

SNAKE

- ☐ green small pom pom
- ☐ black and gray chenille stems
- ☐ 2 tiny wiggle eyes
- ☐ red felt scrap
- ☐ 4 flat round wood beads
- ☐ craft glue

TURTLE

- ☐ green pom pom (1 very large, 1 small and 4 very small)
- ☐ green felt
- ☐ 2 tiny wiggle eyes
- ☐ craft glue

To make the Snake:

1. Cut a 9" piece each of 2 black and 1 gray chenille stems. Twist stems together and bend them into a coiled snake.

2. Slide the beads on the snake's tail, gluing in place as necessary.

3. Freehand cut a tongue from red felt. Glue the tongue and wiggle eyes to the green pom. Glue the green pom to the snake for the head.

To make the Turtle:

1. For the head and the body, glue the very large and small green poms together. For the legs, glue the very small poms to the body.

2. Freehand cut six green felt irregularly shaped circles that are about $^1/_2$" diameter each. Freehand cut a green felt tail. Glue the circles and tail to the body.

3. Glue the wiggle eyes to the head.

SHOPPING LIST

RACCOON

- ☐ tan pom poms (1 very large, 1 large, and 4 very small)
- ☐ tiny rust pom pom
- ☐ tan and dark brown chenille stems
- ☐ 2 tiny wiggle eyes
- ☐ black, tan, and pink felt scraps
- ☐ tracing paper
- ☐ craft glue

SPIDER

- ☐ dark brown pom poms (1 very large and 1 small)
- ☐ 4 dark brown chenille stems
- ☐ 2 tiny wiggle eyes
- ☐ craft glue

To make the Raccoon:

1. For the head and body, glue the large tan pom to the very large tan pom. For the legs, glue the very small tan poms to the body. For the tail, cut a 3" piece each of 2 tan and 2 dark brown chenille stems. Twist stems together and glue to the back of the body.

2. Trace the eye mask pattern onto tracing paper. Use the pattern to cut the mask from black felt. Freehand cut tan felt triangles for the ears. Cut slightly smaller pink triangles for the inner ears.

3. Glue inner ears to ears. Glue eye mask, ears, rust pom for nose, and wiggle eyes to the head.

To make the Spider:

1. For the legs, cut four $6^1/_2$" pieces of chenille stems. Hold all 4 chenille stems together and twist together at the middle. Separate the chenille stems into 4 legs on each side. Shape legs and bend the ends to make feet.

2. For the body, glue the very large pom to the legs. For the head, glue the small pom to the body. Glue the wiggle eyes to the head.

Aliens

SHOPPING LIST

- ☐ assorted pom poms
- ☐ assorted chenille stems
- ☐ assorted wiggle eyes
- ☐ assorted felt
- ☐ craft glue

Be sure to refer to the Size Guides on page 3 before starting your project.

To make the Aliens:

1. *For the dotted alien*, shape chenille stems into feet and glue to a very large pom. For the head, glue a medium pom to the very large pom. For the beak, cut a $1^1/_2$" piece of chenille stem. Fold in half and glue to the head. Glue a medium wiggle eye to the head. Glue tiny poms to the head and body.
2. *For the alien frog*, cut two 2" pieces and two 6" pieces of chenille stem. Bend them into arms and legs. Freehand cut webbed hands and feet from felt. Glue the felt pieces to the arms and legs. Glue the arms and legs to a very large pom. Glue two small poms to the very large pom for the eyes. Glue a medium and a small wiggle eye to the eye poms. Freehand cut a curved felt tongue and glue it under the eyes.
3. *For the large-eyed alien*, freehand cut a webbed foot from felt and glue it to a very large pom. Glue a small wiggle eye to a very small pom. Cut a 2" piece of chenille stem and glue it to the large pom. Glue the very small pom to the other end of the chenille stem. Glue a large wiggle eye to the very large pom.

Butterfly Wand & Crown

SHOPPING LIST

- ☐ 9" x 12" craft foam sheet
- ☐ adhesive back glitter foam sheets (1 for crown or wand)
- ☐ glitter chenille stems
- ☐ chenille stem for butterfly antennae
- ☐ assorted pom poms
- ☐ 6"w tulle
- ☐ acrylic jewels
- ☐ 12" length of $^{3}/_{16}$" diameter dowel for wand
- ☐ craft knife
- ☐ tracing paper
- ☐ stapler (for crown)
- ☐ craft glue

Be sure to refer to the Size Guides on page 3 before starting your project.

To make the Butterfly Wand:

Steps that require an adult have this symbol *.

1. Trace the butterfly pattern (page 13) onto tracing paper and cut out. Use the pattern to cut 2 butterflies from the glitter foam sheet. Remove the paper backing and stick the butterflies together back-to-back.

*2. Use the craft knife to cut 2 slits in the butterfly *(Fig. 1)*. Slide the butterfly on the dowel through the slits and glue in place.

Fig. 1

3. Cut two 9" pieces of tulle. Tie the tulle pieces around the dowel.

4. For the antennae, cut a $2^{1}/_{2}$" piece of chenille stem. Shape the chenille stem into the antennae and glue to the butterfly. Glue poms to the butterfly. Glue a jewel to the tulle knot.

To make the Crown:

1. For the band, cut two $1^1/_2$" x 12" pieces of foam. Trace the crown pattern (page 13) onto tracing paper and cut out. Use the pattern to cut a crown from the glitter foam sheet and the colored foam sheet. Remove the paper backing and stick the crowns together.

2. Glue the 12" long foam band pieces to the crown back *(Fig. 2)*.

Fig. 2

3. Glue glitter chenille stems, poms, and jewels to the crown and band. Staple the band together to fit your head.

Butterfly Wand

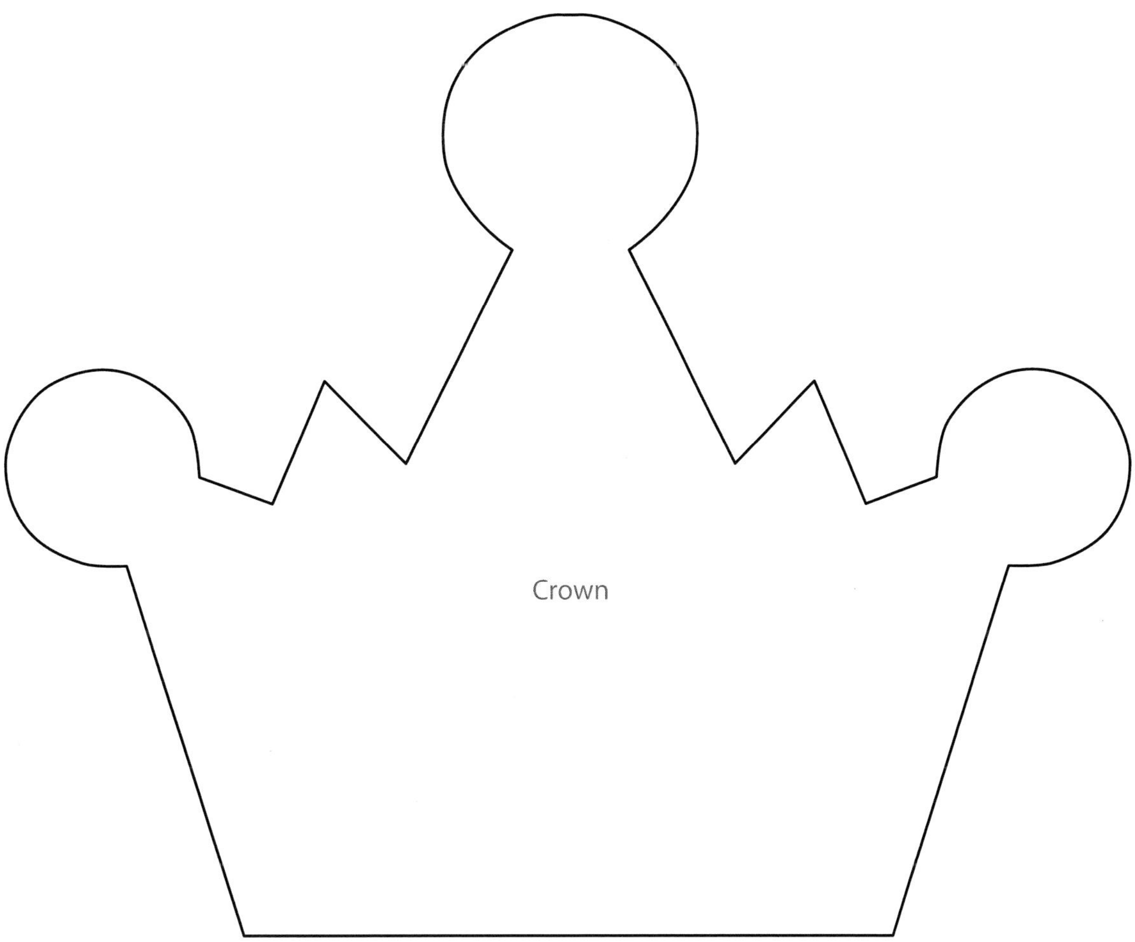
Crown

Inchworm Clip

SHOPPING LIST

- ☐ 2 tiny black pom poms for eyes
- ☐ assorted pom poms (we used 9)
- ☐ lime green felt
- ☐ green chenille stem
- ☐ wood spring-type clothespin
- ☐ black braiding cord
- ☐ tracing paper
- ☐ craft glue

*Be sure to refer to the **Size Guides** on page 3 before starting your project.*

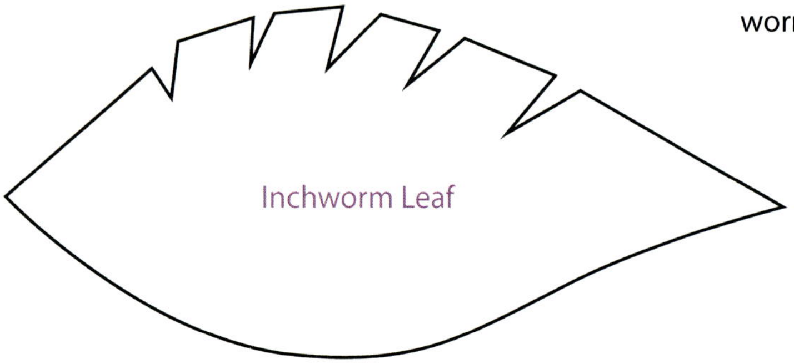

To make the Inchworm Clip:

1. Trace the leaf pattern onto tracing paper; cut out. Use the pattern to cut a felt leaf. Glue the chenille stem to the leaf center. Trim the excess chenille stem.

2. For the antennae, cut a 2$\frac{1}{2}$" piece of braiding cord. Tie a knot close to each end. Fold the cord in half and glue to the pom you want to use for the head. For the eyes, glue the tiny black poms to the head.

3. Glue the head and other poms together to complete the inchworm. Glue the leaf and the worm to the clothespin.

Pom Pom Launcher & Pouch

SHOPPING LIST

- ☐ assorted pom poms for "launching"
- ☐ assorted pom poms to decorate pouch
- ☐ 9" x 12" felt sheets (1 solid color and 1 printed)
- ☐ assorted chenille stems
- ☐ disposable plastic cup that has a 2" bottom diameter
- ☐ 12" round balloon
- ☐ duct tape
- ☐ 31" piece of paracord for strap
- ☐ craft knife
- ☐ craft glue
- ☐ stapler (optional)

Be sure to refer to the Size Guides on page 3 before starting your project.

To make the Launcher:

Steps that require an adult have this symbol ✳.

✳1. Cut the cup about 2 1/2" from the bottom *(Fig. 1)*. Cut a 1 1/4" diameter hole in the bottom of the cup *(Fig. 2)*.

Fig. 1

Fig. 2

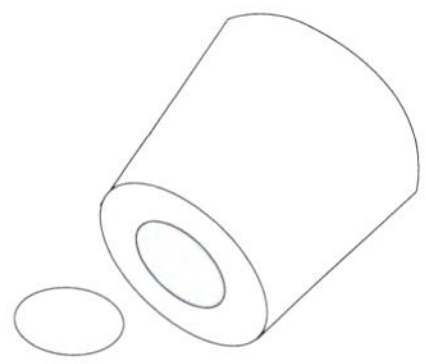

2. Knot the balloon end. Cut the balloon about 4" from the knot. Stretch the balloon and slip it onto the cup, centering the knot under the hole in the cup. Securely tape the balloon to the cup.

3. Launch each pom by dropping it into the launcher, pulling on the balloon knot, and letting go of the knot.

To make the Pouch:

1. Matching the short ends, fold the pouch felt sheet in half. Glue or staple the short sides together. Cut two 1 1/2" x 6" pieces of printed felt. Wrap these pieces over the pouch side edges and glue in place.

2. For the strap, fold each end of the paracord 1 1/2" toward the center. Secure with duct tape, leaving a loop at each end.

3. Cut a 3" piece of chenille stem. Thread it through one loop on the strap. Fold the chenille stem in half and securely glue to one inside corner of the pouch. Repeat with the remaining end of the strap.

4. Shape chenille stems into a "P," "O," and "W". Glue the letters and some poms to the pouch front.

POW

Bookmark

SHOPPING LIST

- ☐ 2 small pom poms for bookworm head and body
- ☐ 3 very small pom poms for bookworm tail
- ☐ 2 tiny wiggle eyes
- ☐ chenille stem for antennae
- ☐ cotton craft thread (2-3 colors)
- ☐ craft glue
- ☐ large-eye hand sewing needle

Be sure to refer to the Size Guides on page 3 before starting your project.

To make the Bookmark:

1. Cut three 15" pieces of craft thread. Thread all 3 strands on the needle and knot the long end.

2. For the head/body, thread a small pom on the craft thread. Glue the remaining small pom to the first pom, covering the thread knot *(Fig. 1)*.

Fig. 1

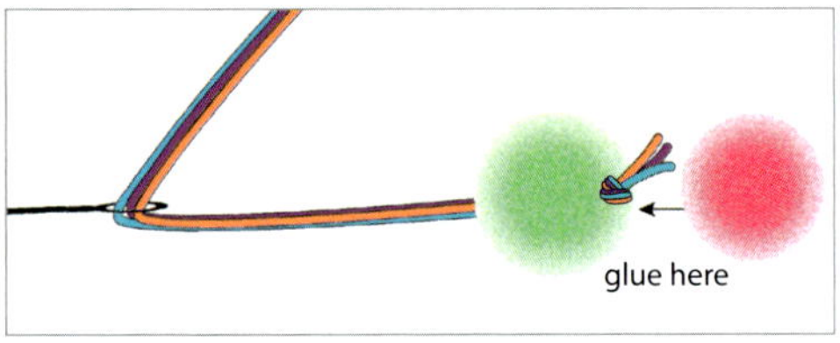

3. For the tail, thread 2 very small poms on the craft thread. Remove the needle and knot the thread close to the end. Glue the remaining very small pom to the tail, covering the thread knot.

4. Glue the eyes to the head.

5. For the antennae, cut two 1/2" pieces of chenille stem. Bend each one close to one end. Glue the straight end to the head.

THE WORLD BOOK
TREASURY OF CLASSICS

Owls

SHOPPING LIST

- ☐ tan pom poms (1 very large and 1 small)
- ☐ rust pom poms (2 small and 2 very small)
- ☐ white pom poms (2 small)
- ☐ brown pom poms (2 tiny)
- ☐ chenille stems (orange, green, tan, and dark brown)
- ☐ wiggle eyes (2 small and 2 tiny)
- ☐ felt (tan and green)
- ☐ small brown feathers
- ☐ tracing paper
- ☐ craft glue

*Be sure to refer to the **Size Guides** on page 3 before starting your project.*

To make the Owls:

1. For the large owl, glue the small rust poms to the very large tan pom. For the beak, cut a 1" piece of orange chenille stem and fold in half. Glue the beak, small eyes, and feathers to the owl. Repeat with the remaining tan and rust poms and tiny eyes to make a baby owl. For the feet, glue the brown tiny poms to the body.
2. For the nest, twist 1 tan and 2 dark brown chenille stems together at one end. Twist the stems and shape into a rounded nest shape ***(Fig. 1)***.

Fig. 1

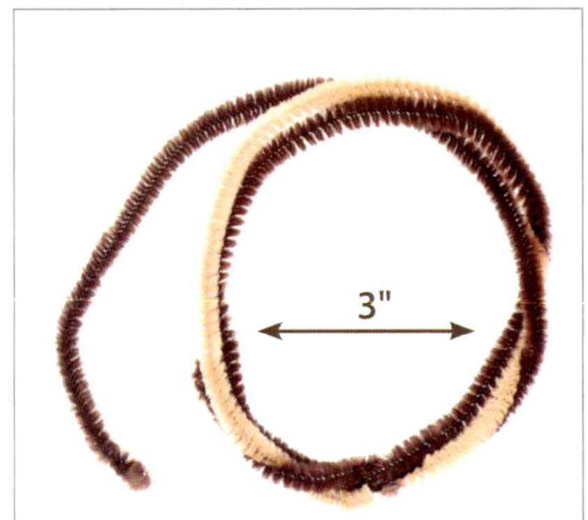

3. Trace the leaf pattern onto tracing paper and cut out. Use the pattern to cut a green felt leaf. Glue a green chenille stem along the outer edges of the felt leaf. Glue the leaf to the nest.
4. Cut a tan felt circle that is about $3\frac{1}{2}$" dia. Push the circle into the nest and glue in place. Glue the baby owl and white poms in the nest.

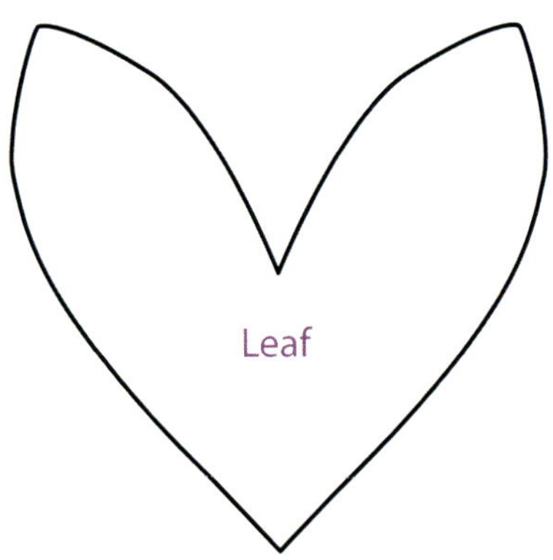

Christmas

SHOPPING LIST

SNOWMAN

- ☐ white pom poms (1 each - large, small, very small, and tiny)
- ☐ black pom poms (3 tiny)
- ☐ 7" length of $^{3}/_{8}$"w green ribbon
- ☐ brown chenille stem
- ☐ felt (blue and red)
- ☐ tracing paper
- ☐ craft glue

ORNAMENT

- ☐ assorted pom poms (red, white, and green)
- ☐ chenille stems (silver glitter and red)
- ☐ red felt
- ☐ acrylic jewel
- ☐ craft glue

ANGEL

- ☐ white chenille stems
- ☐ glitter chenille stems (red and silver)
- ☐ white medium glitter pom pom
- ☐ tiny glitter pom poms (red, white, and green)
- ☐ wood beads for hands and head
- ☐ alphabet beads to spell "PEACE"
- ☐ black permanent marker
- ☐ silver cord for hanger
- ☐ craft glue

TREE

- ☐ chenille stems (lime green and dark green)
- ☐ glitter chenille stems (gold and red)
- ☐ assorted pom poms
- ☐ craft glue

Be sure to refer to the Size Guides on page 3 before starting your project.

To make the Snowman:

1. Freehand cut a 2" diameter blue felt circle. Stack and glue the large, small, and very small white poms together. Glue the snowman to the felt circle. Cut two $^{3}/_{4}$" brown chenille stem pieces. Glue them to the snowman for arms.

2. Trace the hat patten onto tracing paper; cut out. Use the pattern to cut a red felt hat. Roll the felt piece into a cone and glue the straight edges together. Glue the tiny white pom to the hat tip. Glue the hat to the snowman's head. Fold the hat over and glue the fold.

3. Tie the ribbon around the snowman's neck; trim the ends. Glue the black tiny poms to the snowman.

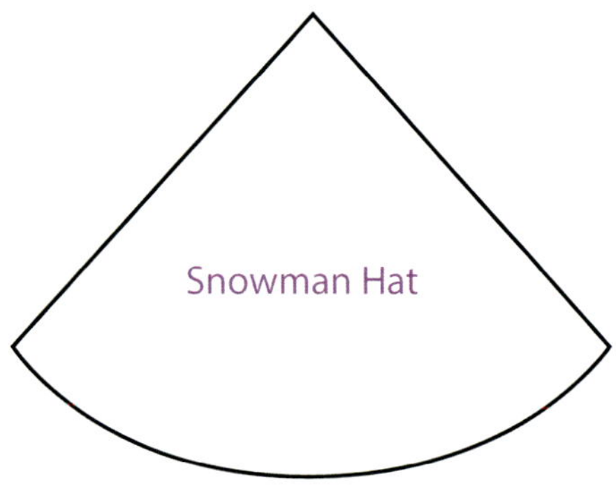

Continued on page 24.

PEACE

Christmas continued

To make the Ornament:

1. Cut a $2^1/_2$" diameter red felt circle. Glue the silver chenille stem around the outer edge of the felt circle, shaping one end into a hook at the top. Glue the poms to the felt circle.

2. Shape a red chenille stem into a bow. Glue the bow to the ornament. Glue the acrylic jewel to the bow.

To make the Angel:

1. For the skirt, cut seven 6" pieces of white chenille stem. Bend six of the pieces into loops. Hold all the loops together. Leaving about 1" on each end untwisted, twist the remaining 6" piece around the tops of the loops. Insert the untwisted ends into the larger bead for the head; add some glue to hold it in place. Arrange the loops into the skirt shape.

2. For the arms, wrap a 4" piece of white chenille stem around the skirt just below the head and extend the ends out to the sides. Wrap a silver glitter chenille stem just below the arms; trim the excess.

3. Shape the wings from a silver glitter chenille stem *(Fig. 1)*. Glue the wings to the angel back.

Fig. 1

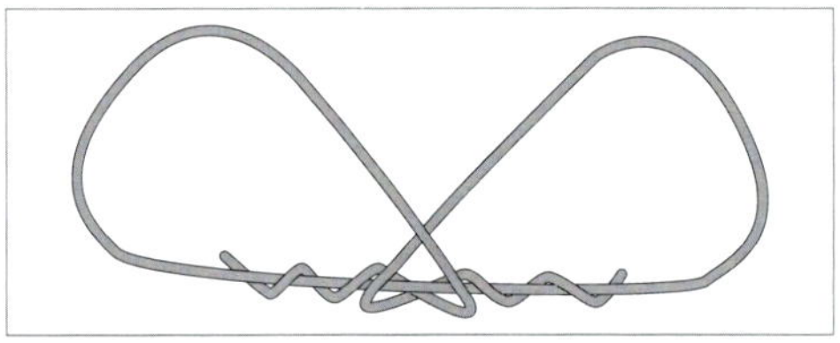

4. Glue the smaller wood beads to the arm ends. Slide the alphabet beads on a red glitter chenille stem. Wrap around the angel's arms, trimming the excess chenille stem.

5. Glue the medium white glitter pom to the head. Draw the eyes on the head.

6. Glue tiny glitter poms to the skirt.

7. For the hanger, cut a 10" long piece of cord. Knot the ends together and glue the knot to the angel back.

To make the Tree:

1. Twist a lime green and a dark green chenille stem together to create a striped chenille stem. Shape the striped stick into a triangle tree shape about 4" high. For the trunk, cut two $2^1/_2$" pieces of lime green chenille stem. Fold each piece in half and glue to the tree bottom.

2. Shape a gold glitter chenille stem into a star and glue to the tree top. Create the garland by gluing pieces of gold glitter chenille stem across the tree. Glue the poms to the garland. Shape red glitter chenille stems into bows and glue to the tree.

Production Team: Technical Editor – Lisa Lancaster; Senior Graphic Artist – Mark Hawkins; Photographer – Rob Karman

Made in U.S.A.